Ibi's Fireflies

KT-415-724

Written and illustrated by Third Grade Students of
Willow Lane Elementary School in Macungie, Pa

cholastic Inc. New York Toronto London Auckland Sydney New Delhi Hong Kong

ORIGINAL COVER

Dedicated to our friend, Ibiyinka Alao. His smile shines brighter than any star!

Ibiyinka Olufemi Alao of Nigeria is the winner of the
United Nations International Art Competition.
He is the United Nations Ambassador of Art.
Ibiyinka was born in Nigeria. We call him "Ibi" for short.
His paintings and stories carry a message of peace and hope.
This book tells the true story of Ibi and his fireflies.

Meet the Authors

Left to right: Aarya Sevak, Kya Vandersluis, Gloria Klees, Olivia Candy, Conor Fisher, Cassandra Doemling, Vanessa Owusu-Anim, Priya Mancheril, Brighton Yu, Lency Tankwa

Ibi visits our classroom.

Rum-pum-pum-pum.

Ibi was born in Nigeria.

Rum-pum-pum-pum.

We dance around Ibi's drum.

Then Ibi tells us a story.

RUM PUM PUM

When Ibi was a little boy, he would count the stars one by one. They fascinated him. He tried to make pictures out of them in his mind.

One evening, Ibi's father drove him home from school. Ibi saw a cluster of fireflies. "Daddy, look at the fireflies." Ibi was surprised when his father stopped the car.

Ibi's father went to the trunk and pulled out a transparent jar.

Ibi and his father picked fireflies and put them in the jar. They were running all over together. This is heaven, Ibi thought. The fireflies twinkled in the jar. It was a beautiful sight.

But then Ibi's father said,
"You must let the fireflies go
now." Ibi frowned. He loved
the fireflies so much. Ibi
wanted to keep them forever.

Ibi's heart felt a little broken. His father gave him a soft pat, "Let the fireflies go or they will die."

Ibi still looked sad because this answer was too simple. His father understood. "If you don't let the fireflies go, you will never see stars in the sky," he said.

"In the middle of the night, fireflies turn into stars.

So if you want to keep seeing stars in the sky, every time you catch a firefly, you must let it go."

Ibi looked at the fireflies in the jar. Then he glanced at the stars in the sky. They both twinkled. They both looked the same.

Ibi believed his father.

So Ibi let the fireflies go free.

After that day, Ibi was still fascinated by fireflies, but he did not want to keep them. Instead, Ibi would carefully push the fireflies back up into the sky.

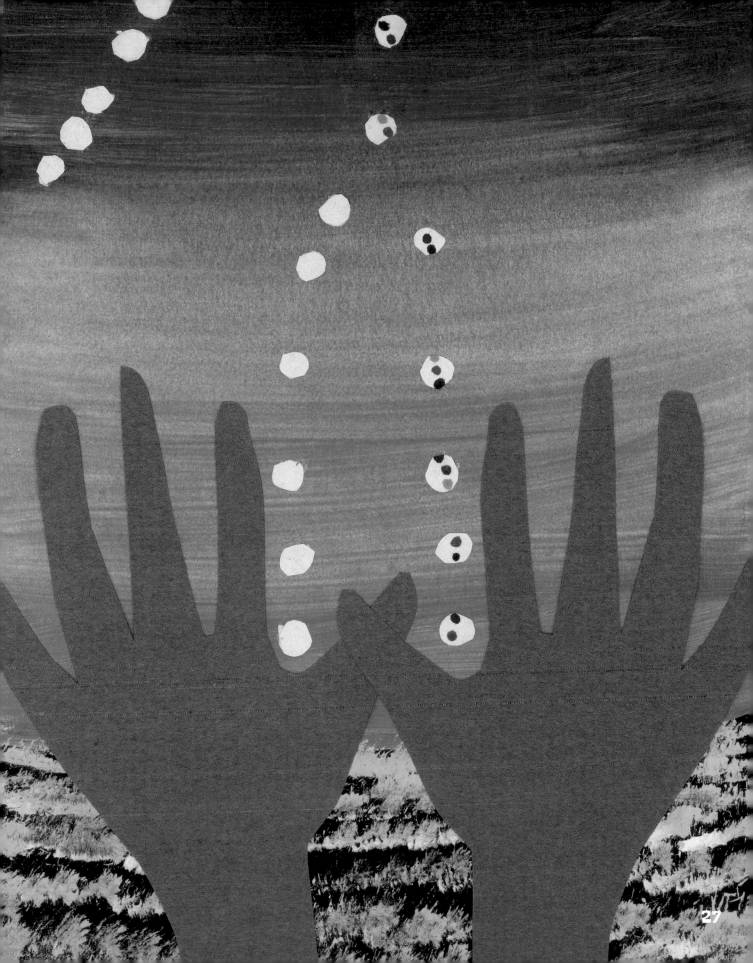

Ibi says, "When you love something as much as I loved those fireflies, the best thing is to let it go free. It will then become a giant star that will shine down on you forever."

Pictures from our day
With Ibiyinka Alao

Ibi tells us the story about his fireflies.

Ibi teaches us to paint just like him with bright colors and dots.

Ibi shows us his painting titled, "Grace: That Even The World Can Pass Through It."

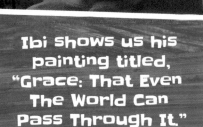

Ibi plays an African song on the drums. We sing and dance.